This Is Not S

Hollywood hype would
tist can stare into your ey
like a zombie, totally und   ly one
example of the misinforma   _n About Hyp-_
nosis clears away so that you   derstand and benefit
from this powerful, natural and completely safe self-
improvement tool, without superstition or fear.

Hypnosis is neither unnatural nor mysterious. The
process of hypnosis simply takes advantage of your own
brain's alpha cycle—a cycle that you experience every
time you go to sleep—to allow you or your hypnotist to
speak directly to your subconscious mind. This method
is an incredibly effective way to cancel out the negative
programming you've accumulated over the course of a
lifetime and replace it with positive messages.

Hypnotic suggestions can aid you by enhancing concentration, confidence, memory, healing, longevity,
weight loss, work success and sexual performance—and
by wiping out depression, phobias, procrastination, poor
habits and other results of negative programming.

Wide-spread ignorance and negative preconceptions
about hypnosis—along with unfounded fears of its sup-
posed dangers—only deprive people of hypnosis' real
benefits and the full quality of life to which everyone is
entitled. _The Truth About Hypnosis_ will open your mind to
this practical tool's countless applications and show you
how you can better your life using the natural powers of
your own mind—easily and safely.

About the Author

William W. Hewitt has devoted most of his adult life to training, teaching, motivating, and counseling people. He lectures and conducts workshops on personal development, and as a certified hypnotherapist, as well as a professional astrologer, has counseled and guided hundreds of people to capitalize on their strengths, overcome problems, and create better lives for themselves. A former IBM executive and non-commissioned Air Force officer, he now spends his time writing both for the public and for private industry.

To Write to the Author

If you wish to contact the author or would like more information about this book, please write to the author in care of Llewellyn Worldwide and we will forward your request. Both the author and publisher appreciate hearing from you and learning of your enjoyment of this book and how it has helped you. Llewellyn Worldwide cannot guarantee that every letter written to the author can be answered, but all will be forwarded. Please write to:

William W. Hewitt
℅ Llewellyn Worldwide
P.O. Box 64383-L365, St. Paul, MN 55164-0383, U.S.A.

Please enclose a self-addressed, stamped envelope for reply,
or $1.00 to cover costs.
If outside U.S.A., enclose international postal reply coupon.

Free Catalog from Llewellyn

For more than 90 years Llewellyn has brought its readers knowledge in the fields of metaphysics and human potential. Learn about the newest books in spiritual guidance, natural healing, astrology, occult philosophy, and more. Enjoy book reviews, new age articles, a calendar of events, plus current advertised products and services. To get your free copy of *Llewellyn's New Worlds of Mind and Spirit*, send your name and address to:

Llewellyn's New Worlds of Mind and Spirit
P.O. Box 64383-L365, St. Paul, MN 55164-0383, U.S.A.

The Truth About

Hypnosis

by William W. Hewitt

1996
Llewellyn Publications
St. Paul, MN 55164-0383, U.S.A.

For permissions, or for serialization, condensation, or for adaptations, write the Publisher.

FIRST EDITION, 1993
SECOND EDITION
First Printing, 1996

International Standard Book Number:
0-87542-365-5

LLEWELLYN PUBLICATIONS
A Division of Llewellyn Worldwide, Ltd.
P.O. Box 64383, St. Paul, MN 55164-0383

Other Books by William W. Hewitt

The Art of Self Talk
Astrology for Beginners
Bridges to Success and Fulfillment
Hypnosis (originally titled *Daydream Your Way to Success*)
Psychic Development for Beginners
Tea Leaf Reading

This book is dedicated to
my friend, Nancy J. Mostad,
who encouraged me with
my writing.

THE BIG PICTURE

There are probably more myths, misconceptions, and misinformation about hypnosis than any other subject. This is due in large part to movies, television, and novels that make no attempt to be truthful in dealing with hypnosis. They are more interested in creating dramatic effect than in presenting truth. Drama sells! Truth doesn't sell. As a result, the public gets fed tons of drama, half-truths, and tons of false information about hypnosis.

This booklet will set the record straight, expose some myths, and explain in simple language what hypnosis is and what it is not.

Myth: The hypnotist can make you do things against your will.

Absolutely false. The hypnotist has no power over you at all and cannot make you do anything against your will. Hypnosis is really just self-hypnosis. All the hypnotist does is guide you into a hypnotic state, which you can easily learn to do for yourself, if you wish. The hypnotist is not a master, but a guide, and does not have any special power or magic.

Myth: You can get stuck in hypnosis and never come out.

False again. If you are hypnotized and the hypnotist left the room and never returned, your own mind would pull you safely out of the hypnosis in one of two ways. You would either realize the

1

hypnotist was no longer talking to you, and you would open your eyes and be wide awake and feeling fine, *or* you would drift into a normal sleep for a few minutes and then wake up normally, feeling fine.

Myth: When hypnotized, you are in a trance and have no control.

Not true. First, hypnosis does not put you into a trance. You are always awake and aware of what is happening. Hypnosis is like a daydream state. You are awake and aware but are very relaxed with your attention focused on a specific thought or image. Second, you always have control. If the hypnotist told you to rob a bank you would just say, "No" and open your eyes. You would not rob the bank. Of course, if you really wanted to rob a bank anyway, then you would follow the suggestion to do so. The point is that it is you, not the hypnotist, who makes hypnosis work or not work.

Myth: Everyone can be hypnotized.

False. I have already told you that no one can be hypnotized against their will. In addition, people with certain mental or neurological conditions cannot be hypnotized. And about one percent of the population cannot be hypnotized for reasons that are not known. However, most people can be hypnotized if they want to be.

Myth: Hypnosis can cure anything or solve any personal problem.

No, hypnosis is not a cure-all. Hypnosis is very powerful and can cure, or aid in the cure, of a great many ailments. Hypnosis can also solve a great many personal problems. At times hypnosis can produce what seems to be miracles. But it is not the answer for everything. Hypnosis is a powerful, natural tool we all have available to us to help improve our lives in a great many ways.

Myth: Hypnosis is dangerous.

Untrue. It is quite the opposite. Hypnosis is safe and natural as will be explained more fully shortly.

Myth: Only weak-minded people can be hypnotized.

Again, false. The contrary is true. It is easier to hypnotize people who are intelligent.

Myth: Deep hypnosis is necessary for good results.

Not true. Any level of hypnosis from light to deep can bring good results.

Forget the Hollywood-type hype that depicts people walking around like zombies under the control of some madman who merely has to look into a person's eyes in order to put them into an alleged hypnotic trance. This is pure mythical, dramatic garbage that has absolutely no basis in fact.

Let's talk about truth. Exactly what is hypnosis, or more accurately, self-hypnosis?

Self-hypnosis is a self-induced, altered state of mental consciousness that allows you to give constructive suggestions directly to your subconscious mind.

More simply put, you cause your brain frequency to slow down to the range of seven to fourteen cycles per second. In that frequency range, your mind is highly susceptible to suggestions or instructions. By giving constructive suggestions to your subconscious mind, you can change your life for the better in many ways.

Here are just a few examples of changes you can make with self-hypnosis: stop smoking; stick to a proper diet; gain self-confidence; improve your memory; learn faster and more effectively; improve your self-image and self-esteem; overcome shyness; hasten your recovery from illness or injury; improve your sexual performance; improve any skill; overcome pain; get rid of headaches; relax and overcome stress; stop bed wetting; get rid of any bad habit such as nail biting, stuttering, etc. The list goes on almost endlessly. You can even use self-hypnosis to experience past life regression.

Your subconscious mind is that part of your mind which is like an obedient servant—it does what you program or tell it to do. The subconscious mind does not think, reason, or rationalize. It does not know the difference between right or wrong or positive and negative. The subconscious mind just does what it is instructed to do. If you tell your subconscious mind you are a good, worthwhile person, it will cause you to be a good, worthwhile person. On the other hand, if you tell it that you are an inferior person, it will cause you to behave like an inferior person.

Children are highly susceptible to suggestion because their brains function primarily in the frequency range where the subconscious mind is exposed and unprotected, so to speak. This is why children learn so quickly; their minds absorb everything at a phenomenal rate.

As a result, children who are praised, properly taught, and encouraged will develop good, healthy self-esteem.

Children who are *put down*, told they are stupid or ugly, and are criticized for everything, will develop poor, unhealthy self-esteem.

Is it any wonder then that we adults have so many problems that need correcting? We are the product of many years of mixed programming—some good, some bad. No two of us are exactly alike.

Self-hypnosis is a tool we can use to straighten out the bad programming. Self-hypnosis works because it is a method of allowing ourselves to adjust the brain frequency of our subconscious area and then reprogram our mind with the information we want. Simply, we overlay the negative programming with positive programming, thus cancelling out the negative programming. It works!

BRAIN FUNCTIONS

To give you a better understanding of the whole process of learning, programming, and physical growth, at this point let's digress briefly to discuss in a more technical way how your brain functions. Then you will be better equipped to understand self-hypnosis and what it can do for you.

The brain operates at various frequencies from time to time in order for us to perform our activities as human beings. On any given day, any person who is not under the influence of certain drugs, or is not in a coma, will experience all of the various brain frequencies. The brain frequency ranges are named delta, theta, alpha, and beta.

Delta

Delta has a frequency range of zero to four approximately cycles per second. This is the range of total unconsciousness.

Theta

The theta range of brain activity is approximately four to seven cycles per second. This is considered to be the psychic range of the mind and the area where psychic experiences occur. All emotional experiences seem to be recorded in this area of brain activity.

Children under seven years old have the predominance of their brain activity in the theta area, although they also experience the other ranges as well. Notice how the physical age closely correlates to the predominant brain frequency range. Children in this age group are highly receptive to having their subconscious minds programmed with suggestions from all sources.

In theta, learning is extremely rapid, and there probably is also a lot of subliminal learning from other dimensions.

In the under seven age group, children often see *imaginary* playmates and talk to them. Perhaps these are not imaginary, but are really a link with another dimension of intelligence. Interesting thought, is it not?

Some hypnosis and some past life regression experiences also occur in the theta range of brain activity.

Alpha

The alpha range of brain activity is approximately seven to fourteen cycles per second. This is considered to be the range of the subconscious mind.

This is the area of brain activity where all nocturnal dreaming and daydreaming takes place. Most past life regression and nearly all hypnosis also takes place in alpha.

Children in the seven to fourteen age group function predominantly in alpha, although they also function in all the other ranges as well. Hence, they are highly receptive to suggestions from all sources. Again, notice the correlation between the physical age and the predominant frequency range of brain activity.

Rapid learning takes place in alpha.

At approximately ten cycles per second of brain activity, the eye lids will flutter somewhat like a nervous twitch. This is called Rapid Eye Movement or R.E.M., for short. If you notice a sleeping person in R.E.M. (with twitching eye lids), you will know they are dreaming because all dreaming takes place in R.E.M.

Beta

The beta range of brain activity is approximately fourteen cycles per second and higher, with an average of around twenty-two cycles per second for most activities.

Beta is the range of the conscious mind where we conduct our daily activities that involve thinking, rationalizing, talking, decision making, interacting with others, etc. If we are awake, over fourteen years old, and doing something, our predominant brain frequency will be in the beta range. Note the age and frequency correlation.

When the brain is operating in beta, it is not especially receptive to suggestions.

Even though each age group has a predominant brain activity range, each group does also use all the other ranges from time to time everyday. This enables us to function as total human beings and to have a full range of experiences.

For example, an executive in a business meeting is functioning primarily in beta, talking, reasoning, arguing, and thinking. After the meeting, the executive retreats back to the office and sits quietly in a chair to relax and allow the data from the meeting to *sink in.* The process of relaxing and allowing the mind to grow quiet causes the brain frequency to automatically slow down to below fourteen cycles into the alpha range. In alpha, the mind quickly absorbs the data from the meeting and files it in the brain for retrieval at some later time.

SLEEP AND DREAMS VS. SELF-HYPNOSIS

When you go to sleep at night, your brain automatically cycles down from the beta range into alpha and then for brief cyclic periods into theta and delta. Then it cycles back up into alpha, where you spend most of your sleep and do all your dreaming.

All hypnosis does is take advantage of this natural phenomenon. Hypnosis is a technique for causing the brain to cycle down into alpha without going to sleep. In alpha, the subconscious mind is open for suggestive input.

The conscious mind does not take suggestion very well. It is most useful for thinking, reasoning, and putting into action those things it already knows.

However, the subconscious mind is like an obedient servant. It doesn't think or reason. It just responds to what it is told. Herein lies the value and power of self-hypnosis. By self-hypnosis, you can pump powerful suggestions directly into your subconscious mind. Your subconscious mind accepts the suggestions and causes them to become reality. In part, it does this by informing the conscious mind that there is new information to be acted upon. The conscious mind loves to act on what it already has, so it starts to act on this new information. In part, we really do not understand why hypnosis works and how the subconscious mind brings about results. We do know that it does work and works quite well.

It is extremely important that all suggestions given during self-hypnosis are positive, constructive, and beneficial. This is because the subconscious mind doesn't know the difference between a good suggestion and a bad suggestion. The subconscious mind merely accepts what you give it and then acts on it.

GENERAL HYPNOSIS TECHNIQUE

All hypnosis does is capture your natural *going to sleep* scenario, while keeping you awake, so you can give your subconscious mind beneficial suggestions.

How does hypnosis do this?

Since the conscious mind, or beta, does not do a very efficient job of absorbing suggestions, the job of hypnosis is to bore the conscious mind so much that it quiets down, stops thinking, and allows the brain to slow down into the alpha range, or the subconscious mind.

In general, this is accomplished by performing a series of physical and mental exercises that bore the conscious mind.

The Usual Approach:

1. Go through two or more physical exercises whereby the subject relaxes every part of the body by following verbal instructions from the hypnotist.

2. Next there are usually two or more visualization exercises which trigger the subconscious mind into creative mental imagery, causing the body to relax even more while lowering the brain frequency.

   Note: The preceding two steps are known as the *hypnotic induction*. The subject may or may not experience R.E.M. or Rapid Eye Movement during the induction, depending on how far through alpha the induction progresses. In any case, it is nothing to be concerned about.

3. Then the beneficial suggestions are given to the exposed subconscious mind. There may be as many or as few

suggestions as desired. The suggestions may be simple or complex. It makes no difference, the subconscious mind can handle it.

4. After the suggestions, there is a short awakening procedure.

Technically it is not an awakening because the subject is not asleep, but merely at a deep level of relaxation. This awakening procedure merely guides the subject slowly back up into beta range, thereby avoiding the subject being startled by suddenly opening his or her eyes while still in alpha. There is no harm if the subject does open his or her eyes while still in alpha, but there could be a moment of confusion. For example, it would be like being awakened in the middle of a deep sleep at night by a loud noise. You open your eyes and are awake, but there are a few moments of disorientation or confusion. The awakening procedure prevents the possibility of this happening.

I have just discussed the general approach to hypnosis. There are, however, many deviations from what I've just described.

With children, for example, the procedure is much shorter because their predominant brain function is already in alpha or theta, and often involves some physical contact, such as touching an arm as a signal, and usually lasts only a few minutes as opposed to twenty or thirty minutes, which is typical for an adult's first hypnosis session.

And once an adult has been hypnotized, subsequent procedures can be made shorter depending on the use of post-hypnotic suggestion and on the susceptibility of the particular subject.

Some people are so receptive to hypnosis that they can be hypnotized in just a few minutes, occasionally in seconds, while others take fifteen to thirty minutes. In general, once a person has been hypnotized, the second time is easier and faster and so on.

Most people can hypnotize themselves easier if they have been previously hypnotized and conditioned by someone else. This previous experience could have been by a tape recording as well as in person.

People can, however, learn to hypnotize themselves without having been previously hypnotized, although there generally is more time and effort needed. A person can make a tape recording of his or her own voice doing a hypnosis procedure and then play it back for self-hypnosis. This can work quite well. Some people do not like to hear their own voice on a recording, in which case they should either purchase some professional hypnosis tapes or have someone they know make the recording.

I mentioned the term *post-hypnotic suggestion*. This refers to a suggestion given under hypnosis that will take place at some later time after the hypnosis session has ended. Here are two examples of post-hypnotic suggestion:

1. "The next time you are hypnotized you will relax ten times faster and go ten times deeper than you are now." This sets the subject up so future hypnosis sessions will be even more successful.

2. "Anytime in the future that you attempt to eat chocolate or other confection you will immediately feel full and nauseous and will not be able to eat it." A suggestion like this might be used for someone who is overweight and who is a compulsive eater of candy.

Hypnotic suggestion usually lasts only about two weeks on average, thus the suggestions need to be repeated and reinforced until such time as the desired result is firmly achieved. On some people, hypnotic suggestion lasts only a few hours or a couple of days. For this reason, hypnotic suggestions should be reinforced every day until permanent success has been achieved.

This is why self-hypnosis is so valuable. You just make a tape recording of your hypnosis procedure and listen to it every day, taking only twenty to thirty minutes, or less, of your time.

If, for example, you want to stop smoking cigarettes you could make or purchase a tape cassette dealing with smoking and just listen to it daily until you have permanently stopped smoking. If at some future time you get strong urges to start smoking again, just get the tape out. Listen to the tape to get rid of the temptation. In the back of this booklet are listings of some hypnosis tapes and books that you might want to consider purchasing in order to pursue self-hypnosis further. This booklet, of course, can only give you the highlights of the subject because it isn't long enough to go into all the details and give complete coverage from all aspects. This booklet is just the tip of the iceberg, so to speak.

Now look at one actual hypnosis procedure. The one selected is the kind most likely to be used in an adult's first hypnosis session.

A TYPICAL HYPNOSIS PROCEDURE

There are literally hundreds of hypnosis routines that can be put together to form a hypnosis procedure. To illustrate a typical procedure, I have organized a few routines in a sequence that is good for general use, relaxation, and for giving beneficial suggestions. The procedure is worded for the hypnotist, sometimes also called the *operator*, to give to another person, called the subject. But it can easily be reworded and administered as self-hypnosis. To give the routine to yourself, simply record the procedure on a cassette tape and then play it back while following the instructions.

I have labeled each routine with a letter or a number and letter combination for easy identification. Of course, you do not say these identifying numbers to the subject. They are provided for easy identification.

Just before starting this particular procedure I give the following brief instruction to the subject:

"In a few moments I am going to ask you to close your eyes and follow my instructions. Shortly after we begin the session, I will ask you on three separate occasions to open your eyes. When I do ask, I really do not want you to open your eyes. I want you to pretend to try to open your eyes by stretching the eyelids, but I do not want you to open them."

Then I will say something like:

"Now relax your eyes, at which time you may stop pretending to try to open them and just relax. Here is what I mean...(at this point I demonstrate what I mean)...Now you try it (I wait for a few moments to allow the subject's eyelids to repeat what I just demonstrated). That was fine. Of course, at the very end of this session I will really want you to open your eyes when I say something like, 'In a few moments I will count from one to five and you will open your eyes and be wide awake.' Do you understand? In the beginning, we will have three brief tests where I do not want you to open your eyes, but at the very end of the session I really do want you to open them. (I wait for the subject to acknowledge that he or she understands. If the subject doesn't understand, I go over it until he or she does). Now let's begin."

Routine A

First I want you to stand up and take a good, complete stretch. Get all the kinks out. (I wait for a few moments while the subject stands up and stretches thoroughly.) That's fine. Now just sit in the chair and relax. Close your eyes and take a nice, deep, full breath and exhale completely, all the way to the bottom of your lungs. All out. Do it again now. Just relax and let it all out. One more time, and this time hold your breath when you have filled your lungs with clean, refreshing, relaxing air. Hold it in. Keep your eyes closed. Now let your breath out slowly and feel yourself relaxing all over.

Routine A-1

Focus your attention on your knees now and relax everything below your knees. Relax your calves. Relax your ankles. Relax your feet. And relax your toes. Everything below your knees now is loose and relaxed. Now relax your thighs as completely as you can. Let your thighs just droop limp, loose and heavy into the chair. Relax your hips, and relax your waist. Now relax your chest as completely as you can.

Allow your breathing to be easier and deeper, more regular and more relaxed. Relax your shoulders now. Let the muscles in your shoulders be heavy and loose, more and more completely relaxed. Relax your neck and throat. Let your head

just droop as all the muscles in your neck just relax.
Now relax your face as completely as you can.
Allow your face to be smooth and loose, relaxed
and easy, your jaws all loose and relaxed, your
teeth are not quite touching. Everything smooth
and loose and easy.

Now relax, as completely as you can, all the little
muscles around your eyelids. Feel your eyelids
growing heavier and smoother, more and more
deeply relaxed.

In a moment, I am going to ask you to open your
eyelids. When I ask you to open them, your eyelids
will be so relaxed and heavy they will just barely
open. When I ask you to close your eyelids again,
you will allow yourself to relax even more completely. Now try to open your eyelids. Now close
your eyes, and feel yourself relaxing even more.

Routine B

I want you to imagine now that all your tensions,
tightness, fears, and worries are draining away
from the top of your head. Let it drain down
through your face, down through your neck,
through your shoulders, through your chest, your
waist, your hips, your thighs, down through your
knees, your calves, your ankles, your feet, and out
your toes. All your tension, tightness, worries, and
fears are draining away now from the very tips of
your toes. You are relaxing more and more.

Routine B-1

We are going to do this relaxation exercise again. This time I want you to allow yourself to relax even more fully and completely than you did the first time.

Focus your attention on your knees once again, and relax everything below your knees. Relax your calves. Relax your ankles. Relax your feet, and relax your toes. And now relax your thighs even more completely. Allow your thighs to droop limp and heavy into the chair. Relax your hips and your waist. Feel the relaxation flowing into your chest now. Relax the vital organs within your chest, your heart, your lungs. Allow your breathing to be more intense, more regular, and more completely relaxed. Now relax your shoulders even more. Feel your shoulders heavy and loose. Feel more and more deeply relaxed. Relax your neck and throat. Relax your face even more. Feel your face all smooth and loose, completely easy and relaxed all over. And now relax, even more, all the little muscles around your eyelids. Feel your eyelids become heavy and smooth. Feel more and more deeply relaxed.

In a moment when I ask you to open your eyelids, your eyelids will be so relaxed, so lazy, that they may not even work. But whether your eyelids open or whether they do not open, in either case when I ask you to close your eyes again you will allow yourself to relax even more completely.

Open your eyelids. Now close your eyes, and feel yourself relaxing even more.

Routine C

We are going to do this relaxation exercise once again. This time I want you to allow yourself to relax completely. There is nothing to fear. You will always hear me. Just pull out all the stops, and allow yourself to sink into perfect relaxation.

Focus your attention again upon your knees and relax everything below your knees. Relax your calves, relax your ankles, relax your feet, and relax your toes. Now relax your thighs completely. Feel the deep and heavy relaxation flowing into your hips now. Feel it going up through your waist, flowing into your chest, to your shoulders, heavy and loose, completely relaxed. Now this heavy, relaxed feeling is going into your neck and throat, all over your face. Your face is all smooth and loose, completely easy and relaxed, and the heavy relaxation is flowing into your eyes and eyelids now. Your eyelids are so heavy and so smooth. Ever more deeply relaxed.

Routine D

In a moment when I ask you to open your eyelids, I want you to believe very, very strongly that your eyelids are glued together. I want you to imagine that your eyelids are like one piece of skin. Don't be antagonistic or skeptical and say that you can open your eyelids. Just believe, just imagine that your eyelids are glued together. And if you believe and if you imagine that you cannot open your eyelids, you will really not be able to open them. Believe now very, very strongly that your eyelids are glued together. Imagine your eyelids are like one piece of skin. Now try to open your eyes. Now let your eyes relax. Feel yourself relaxing all over.

Routine E

I want you to imagine now that you are looking at a blackboard. And on the blackboard is a circle. Into the circle put an X. Now erase the X from inside the circle. And now erase the circle. Forget about the blackboard now as you just go on relaxing more and more deeply.

In a moment, I am going to count backwards from one-hundred. I want you to count with me, silently to yourself. Say each number to yourself as I say it, then when I ask you, erase the number from your mind and allow yourself to relax even more deeply...100...say the 100 to yourself. Now erase it from your mind and go deeper...99...and erase it all away...98...and erase it...97...and now erase it so completely there is nothing left at all, just deeper and deeper waves of relaxation.

Routine F

Focus your attention now on the very tip of your nose. Keep your attention gently focused on the tip of your nose until you reach a point where your entire attention is on my voice. And when you reach that point, you can forget about your nose and just go on listening to my voice and allowing yourself to relax more and more deeply. And as you keep your attention focused very gently on the tip of your nose, I am going to take you down through four progressively deeper levels of relaxation.

Routine G

I will label these levels with letters of the alphabet. When you reach the first level, level A, you will be ten times more deeply relaxed than you are even now. From level A, we will go down to level B. When you reach level B, you will be ten times again more deeply relaxed than you were before. From level B, we will go down even further, down to level C. When you reach level C, you will be ten times again more deeply relaxed than before. From level C, we will go all the way down to the deepest level of relaxation, level D. When you reach level D, you will be ten times again more deeply relaxed than before.

You are drifting down now, two times deeper with each breath that you exhale. Two times deeper with each breath. Your hands and fingers are so relaxed and heavy, and they keep growing heavier.

Feel the heaviness growing in your hands and fingers. Heavy … heavier still until now they are so heavy it is as though your hands and fingers were made of lead. And this deep relaxed, heavy feeling is flowing up through your forearms now. Feel it going up into your upper arms. Flowing through your shoulders, into your neck, over your face, over your eyes. Flowing up to your eyebrows, your forehead, over the top of your head. The deep relaxed, heavy feeling is flowing down the back of your head and down the back of your neck. You are now approaching level A.

Routine H

You are on level A now and still going deeper. Five times deeper now with each breath that you exhale. Five times deeper with each breath. Your mind is so still and peaceful. You're not thinking of anything now. Too relaxed to think. Too comfortable to think. And this heavy relaxation in your mind is flowing into your face and eyes. It is flowing down through your neck and into your chest. Flowing down to your waist, down through your hips, your thighs, your knees, your calves, your ankles, your feet, and your toes. You are now approaching level B.

Routine I

You are on level B now and still drifting deeper. Floating smoothly and gently into perfect relaxation. Your arms and legs are so relaxed and heavy they feel like logs. Your arms and legs are stiff and numb and heavy...simply immovable. Your arms and legs are like planks of wood. You are now approaching level C. You are on level C now and still drifting down. Sinking into the chair. Sinking deeper and deeper into perfect relaxation. And as you go on drifting even deeper, I am going to count backwards from fifteen to one.

Each number that I say will take you deeper and deeper still, and when I reach number one you will be on level D. 15...deeper...14, deeper still, 13...12...11...10...9...8...7...6, let it all go now, 5...4...3...2...1...1...1...so deep, so dreamy, so heavy, so misty. You are now on level D and still drifting down. There is no limit now...no limit. Go on floating, drifting deeper and deeper into perfect relaxation, deeper with each breath.

(At this point, you give your suggestions. If I am using this session as the only session I plan with a client, the suggestions will be as extensive as necessary for the problem being handled.)

Usually this session is just the first of four or six planned for handling of a problem. In this case, I just put in a few general welfare suggestions such as:

1. This is the first of a series of hypnosis session that will enable you to get more control of your life and to enrich your life by solving your problems.

2. Repeat the following statements to your self as I say them: Every day in every way, I am getting better, better, and better.

   3. Positive thoughts bring me benefits and
      advantages I desire.

   You get the idea. You can use the above suggestions, or tailor your own. But you should put in at
least one suggestion, but three would be even better
at this point. Then proceed to the closing, Routine J.

Routine J

The next time I see you, or whenever you hear my
voice on tape, you will allow yourself to relax ten
times more deeply than you are now. And the suggestions I give you then will go ten times deeper
into your mind.

   In a few moments I will awaken you. When you
awaken, you will feel very relaxed and very
refreshed all over. You will feel alive and alert, very
refreshed. Full of energy. You will feel just wonder-
ful. You will keep on feeling relaxed and fine all the
rest of today, and all this evening. Tonight when
you are ready to go to sleep, you will sleep just like
a log all night long. The first thing you know it will
be morning, and you will awaken feeling on top of
the world.

   I am now going to count from one to five. At the
count of five, you will open your eyes, be wide
awake and feeling fine, feeling relaxed, refreshed,
alert, and in very high spirits—feeling terrific!

1...2...coming up slowly now...3...at the count of five you will open your eyes, be wide awake and feeling fine, feeling better than before...4...5. Here I usually snap my fingers at the count of 5 and say: "Open eyes, wide awake and feeling fine, feeling better than before, and this is so!"

Things to Note About this Procedure

Look over routines A-1, B-1, and C. At a quick glance, they seem to be the same. A closer look reveals subtle differences in the wording; these differences are very important. We progress from telling the subject to relax, to feel the relaxation, to you are now relaxed.

In routine J, I have put in "or whenever you hear my voice on tape." If you are not going to tape any sessions, you can leave this out. If you think you may be wanting to perform relaxation over the telephone, then also put in "or whenever you hear my voice on the telephone." Here we are pre-conditioning our subject for future sessions.

A More Complex Situation

Hypnosis quite often can be more complex and creative than the procedure just illustrated. Often it is necessary to have the subject engage in elaborate, realistic visualization. Here are the highlights of one such case I had. I call it my *popcorn case*.

An overweight lady came to me for diet control. Her problem was that she was a compulsive popcorn eater. She bought her popcorn in 100 pound bags. She ate it morning, noon, and night and in between times. The popcorn was always soaked to the point of dripping with real butter and loaded with salt. Of course, to accompany the popcorn, she drank cases of soda pop. I knew that the butter, salt, and soda pop were far more detrimental to her than the popcorn, but popcorn was the vehicle. Without the popcorn, she wouldn't be consuming all those other things. So I decided to make popcorn undesirable to her.

Before hypnotizing her, I tried to find out what she didn't like. She loved everything.

"Isn't there something in life you find repulsive?" I asked in desperation.

"Well, yes. Wet chicken feathers make me ill. I can't stand the smell. My father used to make me kill and pluck chickens against my will."

There I had my mechanism...wet chicken feathers. When I had her into the part of the procedure where I give suggestions, I said, "There is a large bowl of popcorn in front of you. The popcorn has been soaked in wet chicken feathers. The popcorn smells like wet chicken feathers. The popcorn tastes like wet chicken feathers. Now, pick up a kernel of popcorn and put it into your mouth and taste it."

She immediately began to gag and retch. I thought she was going to vomit.

After she left my office she went home and made a batch of popcorn out of habit. This time she did vomit. She tried daily to make popcorn but got nauseous just trying to make it. By the time she came back for session three she had stopped trying to make popcorn. She had kicked the habit, and she was losing excess weight. Of course, without the popcorn, she stopped drinking soda pop, and eating large amounts of butter and salt.

By session six, she had lost around twenty pounds and was looking and feeling good. I had her add more fruit and vegetables to her diet. She was no longer a "popcorn-aholic."

The lesson to be learned here is to find out what tastes or smells are especially offensive to your subject. Use those tastes and smells to remove the desire for the offending eating habit. Most often, the dietary habit that is causing the problem is chocolate, sweets, pastries, etc. If your subject eats five pounds of chocolate a day and she hates the taste of liver, then have her visualize getting some chocolate from the refrigerator where it has been lying next to five pounds of unwrapped wet liver. The liver taste and smell has impregnated all the chocolate, etc. You get the idea.

A Simpler Situation:

Children don't need such lengthy procedures because their brain activity is already predominantly in alpha. It is much easier and faster to induce hypnosis in children; the younger they are, the faster they respond, and the shorter the procedure needed. Also, their attention span is such that they won't listen to a lot of boring words.

Hypnosis for children often makes use of physical contact, such as momentarily touching their forehead or hand to signal them to do something. A small book could be written comprised of just routines for children; perhaps one is already written, but I am not aware of it. I have included some of these quick procedures in my book *Hypnosis*, where I go into extensive detail concerning every aspect of hypnosis.

I also use these quick children's routines quite effectively on adults whom I have previously hypnotized and on those who have a very short attention span due to some sort of infirmity. Quick routines are also excellent for relieving pain or anxiety in an emergency situation.

HOW TO PERFORM HYPNOSIS

First you must either have the hypnosis routines memorized or have them typed and handy so you can easily read them.

Next come a myriad of things to consider: tone of voice; pace of speech; where to position yourself and your subject; lighting conditions; noise conditions; background sounds; where to do it; should any sessions be recorded on tape; use of external equipment; what to observe in your subject; testing for results.

Tone and Pace

Just use the voice you were born with. That may sound like a stupid statement, but it really isn't. I have seen many beginning hypnotists deliberately try to alter their voices when performing, to try to have a more resonant, deep, theatrical sound. This is nonsense. Your normal speaking voice is just fine. A beautiful, melodic, resonant voice is certainly an asset, but it is by no means necessary. It is far more important that you know what you are doing and that you have a good rapport with and respect for your subject.

You do need to give some thought and practice to the pace of your speech. The speech pattern needs to be slow enough to give the subject time to respond to your directions and yet fast enough to retain his or her attention and interest. If you go too slow, the subject's mind will most likely wander to other thoughts. You want to maintain the subject's attention to your voice. You will find that some people need a faster pace while others need a slower pace. Experience will help you find just the right pace.

A pause of two to five seconds is a good average. For example: "Relax your knees" (two second pause). "Relax your calves" (two second pause). "And now relax your toes" (one second pause). "Relax your toes" (two second pause).

In some visualization routines, you may need longer pauses. For example: "I want you to imagine now that you are standing at the top of a spiral staircase" (three second pause). "Create the staircase" (three second pause). "It is carpeted. Create the carpet" (three second pause). You get the idea.

Do not use your watch for timing these pauses. If you do, you probably will get so concerned with time that you will lose track of what you are doing. Just develop a feel for the timing. When I conduct hypnosis, I perform the instructions myself as I give them, thereby keeping a comfortable pace.

Speak in a rather dull, monotonous voice. The idea is to bore the subject's conscious mind to the point that it stops being active, allowing the subconscious mind to be accessible and receptive to your suggestions. If there is too much inflection or drama in your voice, the subject's conscious mind tends to retain interest, thus remaining active and thwarting your goal of deep relaxation and susceptibility to suggestion.

Physical Positioning

I have performed hypnosis while sitting and while standing. I have had subjects who were reclining in recliner chairs, sitting in straight-backed chairs, lying in bed, lying on the floor, sitting cross-legged on the floor, sitting in the front passenger seat of a car while I sat in the back seat, and even while they were standing. All positions work fine, but not necessarily for all situations. For example, a quick two-minute procedure to relieve pain works fine on a person who is standing up. But a thirty minute procedure for diet control is out of the question for a person who is standing up.

Given a choice, the recliner chair or straight-backed, armless chair are the best for the subject. They are equally good. Both offer sufficient comfort and support, and the subject will rarely drift into sleep in either of these.

However, for self-hypnosis, I much prefer to be in a straight-backed, armless chair. These are my personal preferences. As the operator, I also prefer a straight-backed, armless chair.

Lying in bed also offers comfort and support for the subject. The drawback here is that the subject might easily drift into sleep. This is because the body and mind have been conditioned every day that when you lie down, and your brain reaches alpha, you go to sleep. This is the normal sleep process we all go through every night. A skilled operator can usually avoid this situation. When you are working with bedridden people, this is the physical position you must deal with.

Lying on the floor has the same drawback as lying in bed. The subject is more likely to fall asleep. In addition, the floor tends to become uncomfortable rather quickly, so I do not recommend it for lengthy procedures.

Sitting cross-legged on the floor also tends to become uncomfortable rather quickly, so I do not recommend it for lengthy procedures. I use this position quite often for myself for meditation—a form of self-hypnosis—and have had excellent results. I once was in deep meditation for one and half hours in this position without having any physical discomfort. I doubt that an untrained, unskilled person could do that and still be able to get up, much less walk.

Typically, my subject will be in a recliner chair. I will be sitting in a straight-backed chair facing the subject. The distance between us might be from two to six feet. There may or may not be a table or desk between us; this isn't important one way or the other. I need to be close enough so I can speak normally and be easily heard, yet far enough away to not intimidate the subject. There are some procedures I use for special occasions that require me to stand immediately in front of the subject or even have physical contact with the subject. These are the exception, not the rule.

Ideally, the subject's chair should be placed so no bright light falls on his or her eyes. Have windows, unless heavily draped, to the subject's back. The same for electric lights...to the back. This makes it easier for the subject to relax and be comfortable.

Where to Conduct Hypnosis

Most anywhere works fine. I've operated in dimly lit rooms and in bright sunlight outdoors. I've operated in quiet and in noise. The ideal is a quiet, comfortable room with subdued lighting.

If unplanned distractions occur, use them to your advantage. Once I had just begun the hypnosis induction, when a carpenter in the adjacent office began hammering nails in the wall right by my subject's head. It was a staccato bang, bang, bang, bang. I quickly abandoned my usual induction routine and improvised. I said, "Outside noises will not distract you. In fact outside noises will help you to reach a deeper, healthier state of relaxation." Then as each bang occurred I said, "Go deeper" (bang) "deeper" (bang) "deeper and deeper" (bang), etc. My subject went into deep relaxation as though she was on a fast downward elevator. I didn't even need to continue with the remainder of my planned routines. I immediately began giving the suggestions and then brought her out. The results were excellent.

What About Background Music?

Many hypnotists regularly have soothing music or a special tape of the ocean's surf playing in the background while they perform the induction. I have tried both sounds and found them to be satisfactory. However, I have just as satisfactory results without the background sound and I rarely use it. It is just a personal preference. Try it both ways and see which you prefer.

Auxiliary Equipment

All you really need is an inexpensive, portable, AC/DC cassette recorder. I use this only to record one of the induction procedures while I am giving it. I then give the tape to the subject to keep.

If you decide you want background sounds, then you will need the equipment for that.

Some hypnotists use an electric shock device to condition their subjects. For example, during the suggestion phase of the procedure the operator might say, "Imagine now that you are smoking a cigarette. Take a deep drag." (Then the hypnotist would press the button and give the subject an electrical shock). This way the subject equates smoking to a painful experience.

Result

He or she stops smoking. I am fanatically opposed to such procedures and devices. They can be dangerous and harmful. And they are totally unnecessary. A good hypnotist can achieve the same result without resorting to such unacceptable measures. I once took over an office that already had one of these machines. I refused to accept it as part of the inventory and wouldn't sign until it had been physically removed from the premises. My advice: *AVOID ANY SUCH APPARATUS COMPLETELY!* They are bad news!

Observing the Subject

The key items you look for are breathing patterns and muscle tone. As the subject slips into deep relaxation, breathing will be easy and rhythmic. There will be an occasional very deep breath with easy exhaling.

Watch the hands of your subject. Are they gripping the arms of the lounger...fidgeting...twitching? Or are they resting without apparent tension?

The head should droop as the neck muscles relax. The jaw should slacken. There should be no signs of muscle strain or tension.

The eyelids may flutter. This is not tension but rather an indication that the subject is in a state called R.E.M., or rapid eye movement. This state occurs at about ten cycles per second of brain activity, which is well within the alpha range. So if you observe R.E.M., you know for sure that your subject is in hypnosis. The subject can be in hypnosis without R.E.M., so don't be concerned if you do not observe R.E.M.

In general, look for signs of relaxation to indicate that the subject is in hypnosis. Signs of nervousness or tension indicate the subject probably is not in hypnosis, or at most only on the edge of hypnosis.

Do not get overly concerned if a subject doesn't appear to be relaxing very much. No two people react exactly the same way to hypnosis. Just keep on executing your hypnosis routines; they will work in all but a few cases.

I have had subjects who became as limp as wet dish rags within moments after I've started the induction. Others have fidgeted through most of the first session before relaxing only slightly. A few didn't really start to relax until the second session.

I have had only one subject that I was unable to hypnotize. After three sessions, she was still as tense and high strung as a mouse walking through a room filled with hungry cats. I gave her a complete refund and sent her to a colleague. My colleague had the same unsatisfactory results.

The best indicator of responsiveness to hypnosis is to question the subject about it after you have brought them out of hypnosis. The subject will tell you whether he or she was relaxed or not and exactly what was experienced. Of course, final results are the absolute indicator. If you are hypnotizing to stop smoking, and the subject stops, you know you performed your skill correctly and the subject was responsive.

Testing

Some hypnotists perform little tests during the induction to see if it is working. For example, they might tell the subject to try to raise his or her arm just after saying "Your arm is like a log...stiff...immovable." If he or she raises the arm, the subject isn't under hypnosis yet. If he or she doesn't raise the arm, the induction has produced some level of hypnosis.

I do not do testing at all. My theory is that testing creates a doubt in the subject's mind. "Isn't he sure about what he is doing?" "Maybe I am not a good hypnosis subject?" "Will it work or not?" etc.

Even a more pragmatic view...What are you going to do if the test fails and the subject does raise the arm? The only thing you can do is continue the induction which you were going to do anyway.

My approach is one of confidence—the induction does work—and accordingly, it does work.

PRACTICAL APPLICATIONS

What are some of the practical applications for self-hypnosis? The four most widespread uses are:

1. Stop smoking
2. Weight control—i.e. adhere to a proper diet
3. Relaxation and stress management
4. Self-image improvement, which in my judgment is the most valuable of uses.

Examples of Other Possible Uses:

1. **Overcome Phobias:** Fear of height; fear of flying; fear of fire; fear of enclosed places; fear of darkness; fear of anything. This is a valuable use of self-hypnosis.

2. **Business and Work Situations:** Gain self-confidence; improve memory; overcome shyness; tone down over-aggressiveness; learn manners; become more-sociable; etc.

3. **Group Situations:** Overcome stage fright; learn to speak comfortably and effectively in front of a group; learn to be at ease in a group; learn to speak up.

4. **Elderly People:** Overcome feelings of uselessness; learn to feel worthwhile and important; overcome aches and pains; deal effectively with frustrations; learn to live life to the fullest at any age; open your creative mind more fully.

5. **Injury and Healing:** Speed our healing processes.

6. **Habit Control:** Eliminate any undesireable habit—nail biting; picking your nose; being rude, etc. Establish any good habit—being on time for appointments; saying Thank You, etc.

7. **Prison Inmates:** Put your mind to constructive endeavors; create a better attitude; enhance skills; and much more.

8. **Handicapped Persons:** Learn to overcome your handicap and develop your abilities to their greatest potential.

9. **Consult with Higher Power:** This is a spiritual experience that can be phenomenal. Self-hypnosis opens the door to communication with Higher Power.

10. **Shut-Ins:** Learn to use your mind to pass time in a constructive way using self-hypnosis. Get rid of the bad weather blahs by creating your own Sun within your spirit.

The preceding uses of self-hypnosis are just the tip of a very large iceberg. Self-hypnosis is literally the key that can unlock nearly any door you wish.

The only limits to your use of self-hypnosis are the limits you choose to set yourself. Otherwise, the sky is the limit.

For some of you, the *buddy* system will offer the greatest of possibilities and enjoyment. This is where you and a buddy, or buddies, use hypnosis among yourselves on each other. In this way you all learn together at a faster pace, and have the enjoyment of sharing and participating in each others successes.

CASE HISTORIES

You can run into all sorts of unexpected situations that hypnosis can help you resolve. Here are two— out of hundreds—of my cases that you may find interesting. They are excellent illustrations of the power of hypnosis.

Cut Chin Case

In this case, I was both the operator and the subject. It illustrates how self-hypnosis can be valuable in an emergency.

My wife and I were vacationing at the lake one summer, spending most of our time out on our nineteen-foot power cruiser. This particular day we had been lying at anchor, and I walked out onto the bow to pull in the anchor so we could get under way. I slipped on the bow and fell, hitting the point of my chin hard on the metal bow rail.

When I pulled myself up into a sitting position, blood was pouring down my chest from my chin.

My wife's face was ashen. "My God!" she screamed, "I can see the bone!" I immediately pinched the wound shut as hard as I could. As I sat there on the bow, I closed my eyes and almost instantly altered my state of consciousness. In retrospect, I think I probably went all the way down into theta.

I visualized my chin in perfect condition. I bathed it in white, healing light and mentally said, "No bleeding. No pain. No scar. No infection. No swelling. Just perfect healing at one thousand times my normal healing rate." I sat there for perhaps five minutes, pinching the wound shut, while I remained in an altered state with eyes closed. I maintained the vision of a perfect chin while mentally repeating the words several more times.

Then I brought myself out and opened my eyes. I stopped pinching the wound.

There was no more bleeding. A blood scab had formed. It didn't hurt. My wife wanted to return to shore to cleanse and dress my chin. I said no, I was OK. We got under way and enjoyed several hours of boating before going ashore.

When I awakened the next morning, I found that the blood scab had come off during the night. The only reminder of the accident was a thin, red pencil-like line about an inch long on my chin. Within a week, even this pencil line was completely gone. No evidence of the accident was left. And at no time was there pain or swelling.

Cut Foot Case

A young client came in for her appointment on crutches and wearing a cast on her lower left leg and foot. A couple days previously she was running barefoot in her yard and stepped on something that lacerated the bottom of her foot to the bone from toe to heel. She told me how many stitches the doctor had to put in and that he told her she would be in the cast for at least three weeks and perhaps longer and that she probably wouldn't be able to wear a shoe on that foot for several more weeks after the cast was removed.

She was coming to me for diet control, so I hypnotized her and performed the diet control suggestions. She was one of the most receptive hypnosis subjects I have ever had; I could practically hypnotize her by just saying "Close your eyes and relax." She responded just marvelously.

So before I brought her out, I took her through a procedure and suggestions very similar to what I had done to myself three years earlier when I had cut my chin as related in the case just discussed.

The next week she returned for her next appointment without crutches, without a cast on her leg, and she was wearing high heeled shoes. She took off her left shoe to show me the bottom of her foot. There was a thin, red line from toe to heel and that was all. No swelling or discoloration. The wound was healed.

But this story has a punch line, and she was bursting to tell me. She had gone to her doctor the day after the hypnosis session and insisted that he remove the cast. He refused, and a heated argument ensued. She vowed to take a hammer and break it off herself. To save her potential injury from doing it herself, the doctor reluctantly removed the cast. But he warned her it was at her own risk, was going to cost her more money, etc. She said the look on his face was priceless when he saw a healed foot.

"I don't understand," he muttered. Then the young lady told him about the hypnosis session.

The doctor became furious. "I thought you had more sense than to go to quacks!" he scolded. "Obviously, you don't trust me to be your physician. Consider this your last visit to my office. Find yourself another doctor, or should I say find a quack!"

Unruffled, the young lady asked, "Doctor, how do you explain the healing?"

"Obviously, I misdiagnosed it!" he snorted, leaving the examining room. I've often wondered how you can misdiagnose a lacerated foot.

This case does illustrate very vividly the blind, fanatical opposition that does exist against hypnosis in the minds of some people. People tend to oppose anything they do not understand.

Our role as hypnotists is not to meet these opponents in head to head confrontation, but rather to provide patient, knowledgeable education about hypnosis. Most importantly, provide our services with integrity, honesty, and sensitivity. First learn your skill well, then practice it with honor.

The purpose of this booklet is to provide truth and hopefully shed light where there is presently darkness. Ignorance and superstition are terrible things because they rob people of the full quality of life to which they are entitled.

SAMPLE SUGGESTIONS

What follows is just a mini-sample of possible suggestions for various purposes to give you an idea of what hypnotic suggestion is all about.

For Auras

Your aura radiates from you with the strength and colors that you decide by your mental, physical, and emotional condition. You choose to be in such a positive, healthy, balanced state that your aura is powerful, clear, and brilliant with the beneficial energy you desire.

For Concentration

You will feel a tremendous drive and concentration power with everything you do.

For Depression

You will not allow anyone or anything to determine how you are going to feel. You are in control. You choose to feel happy, important, and worthy.

For Drinking

You have made a decision to not drink alcohol. You will feel free of the desire to drink alcohol, and you will not drink it.

For Group Confidence

You will push yourself to meet people. You will take the initiative. You will feel the drive to go out and meet people, and you will start the conversation with ease.

For Healing

You can promote healing in any area of your body by visualizing that area to be flooded in healing, white light, and visualizing the area to be normal and healthy.

For Language Study (insert the language desired)

When you study (Spanish) you will intensely concentrate as you study, and you will remember all the (Spanish) you have studied.

For Longevity

You are what you think. You are now commanding your mind to always direct you to lead your life in such a manner as to promote a long, healthy, happy life. And you will listen to and follow the beneficial dictates of your mind.

For Love and Trust

You will not categorize or stereotype people as being like other people you have experienced because you realize inherently that they are not like other people.

For Memory

Your mind will be like a soft, absorbent sponge and everything you concentrate on you will absorb like a sponge. When you want to remember what you have thought about, you will squeeze your mind like a sponge and you will remember everything you have concentrated on.

For Miscellaneous

Positive thoughts bring you benefits and advantages you desire.

For Money Management

The words bargain and sale no longer entice you. You realize those words are used by someone else to get your money. You purchase only what you truly need, and you do not allow merchants to decide what you need or want.

For Physical Exercise

You will have the desire to physically exercise. You will find time each day to physically exercise, and you will exercise your body vigorously. When you have done this, you will feel simply great.

For Phobias (insert your phobia)

You will feel relaxed and at ease (in an airplane). You will feel relaxed, confident, and you will be free of fear.

For Procrastination

You will not put off doing the things you have to do. You will organize the things you have to do, and you will do them to get them out of the way.

For Reading

You will read faster and better comprehend everything you read.

For Time Management

You are now making a commitment to yourself to not put off until tomorrow what can and should be done today.

For Self-Confidence

Never again will you be a slave to anything, to any person, or to any job. You are your own person, and you are in total control.

For Sexual Performance (for a Female)

When you have sexual relations, you will feel relaxed. You will reach a climax.

For Sexual Performance (for a Male)

When you have sexual relations, you will feel relaxed. You will achieve erection and ejaculation.

For Sleep

When you go to sleep this evening you will quickly drop off into a deep, sound sleep for eight hours. The next thing you know it will be daylight, and you will awaken refreshed and alert.

For Smoking

Regardless of what happens at work, you will feel relaxed. You will feel free of the desire to smoke the entire working time.

For Weight Loss

You will feel satisfied with very small quantities of food, and these small quantities of food will satisfy you completely.

For Work Success

You will handle all situations on the job in a very relaxed, calm, and sensible manner, free of tension.

From these few suggestions, you can begin to see the scope and power of self-hypnosis. You can literally alter your life in any way you desire by merely giving yourself the proper suggestions using self-hypnosis.

SUMMARY

- Self-hypnosis is a procedure that bores your conscious mind to the point where it grows quiet, allowing you to speak directly to your subconscious mind.

- Your subconscious mind, being an obedient servant, does what you tell it to do.

- Self-hypnosis is safe and natural because all it does is take advantage of the *going to sleep cycle* that we all experience every time we go to sleep.

- Self-hypnosis is a powerful tool available to all of us that can provide us a way to alter our lives in virtually any manner we choose.

This booklet provides an excellent overview of hypnosis. There is, however, much more to be learned and experienced for those of you who wish to pursue the subject further. See this author's books and tapes listed elsewhere in the booklet.

On the following pages you will find listed, with their current prices, some of the books now available on related subjects. Your book dealer stocks most of these and will stock new titles in the Llewellyn series as they become available. We urge your patronage.

TO GET A FREE CATALOG

To obtain our full catalog, you are invited to write (see address below) for our bi-monthly news magazine/catalog, *Llewellyn's New Worlds of Mind and Spirit*. A sample copy is free, and it will continue coming to you at no cost as long as you are an active mail customer. Or you may subscribe for just $10 in the United States and Canada ($20 overseas, first class mail). Many bookstores also have *New Worlds* available to their customers. Ask for it.

TO ORDER BOOKS AND TAPES

If your book store does not carry the titles described on the following pages, you may order them directly from Llewellyn by sending the full price in U.S. funds, plus postage and handling (see below).

Credit card orders: VISA, MasterCard, American Express are accepted. Call us toll-free within the United States and Canada at 1-800-THE-MOON.

Postage and Handling: Include $4 postage and handling for orders $15 and under; $5 for orders *over* $15. There are no postage and handling charges for orders over $100. Postage and handling rates are subject to change. We ship UPS whenever possible within the continental United States; delivery is guaranteed. Please provide your street address as UPS does not deliver to P.O. boxes. Orders shipped to Alaska, Hawaii, Canada, Mexico and Puerto Rico will be sent via first class mail. Allow 4-6 weeks for delivery. **International orders:** Airmail – add retail price of each book and $5 for each non-book item (audiotapes, etc.); Surface mail – add $1 per item.

Minnesota residents add 7% sales tax.

Llewellyn Worldwide
P.O. Box 64383-L365, St. Paul, MN 55164-0383, U.S.A.
For customer service, call (612) 291-1970.

Prices subject to change without notice.

PSYCHIC DEVELOPMENT FOR BEGINNERS
An Easy Guide to Releasing and Developing Your Psychic Abilities
William Hewitt

Psychic Development for Beginners provides detailed instruction on developing your sixth sense, or psychic ability. Improve your sense of worth, your sense of responsibility and therefore your ability to make a difference in the world. Innovative exercises like "The Skyscraper" allow beginning students of psychic development to quickly realize personal and material gain through their own natural talent.

Benefits range from the practical to spiritual. Find a parking space anywhere, handle a difficult salesperson, choose a compatible partner, and even access different time periods! Practice psychic healing on pets or humans—and be pleasantly surprised by your results. Use psychic commands to prevent dozing while driving. Preview out-of-body travel, cosmic consciousness and other alternative realities. Instruction in *Psychic Development for Beginners* is supported by personal anecdotes, 44 psychic development exercises, and 28 related psychic case studies to help students gain a comprehensive understanding of the psychic realm.

1-56718-360-3, 5-¼ x 8, 216 pp., softcover $9.95

SELF-HYPNOSIS AUDIOTAPES
by William Hewitt

Change your subconscious in a safe, easy way. Use these tapes in the comfort of your own home to change your life for the better—permanently!

Your Perfect Weight Through Self-Hypnosis

Change the behaviors responsible for unwanted weight gain. William Hewitt offers hypnosis techniques to help you get the body you want!
0-87542-338-8, 45 min. **$9.95**

Become Smoke Free Through Self-Hypnosis

Non-smoker. Easy to say, but it can seem impossible to do. This tape helps you get to the roots of why you smoke, and helps you break the nicotine habit.
0-87542-339-6, 45 min. **$9.95**

Relaxation/Stress Management Through Self-Hypnosis

Stress has been named as a leading cause of many health problems including depression and heart disease. While you can't eliminate stress completely, through self-hypnosis you can learn to control it before it takes its toll on you.
0-87542-335-3, 45 min. **$9.95**

The Psychic Workout Through Self-Hypnosis

Rid your mind of negative feelings, and fill it with positive using this winning combination of self-hypnosis and creative visualization.
0-87542-340-X, 60 min. **$9.95**

Prices subject to change without notice.

HYPNOSIS
A Power Program for Self-Improvement,
Changing Your Life and Helping Others
by William W. Hewitt

There is no other hypnosis book on the market that has the depth, scope, and explicit detail as does this book. The exact and complete wording of dozens of hypnosis routines is given. Real case histories and examples are included for a broad spectrum of situations. Precise instructions for achieving self-hypnosis, the alpha state, and theta state are given. There are dozens of hypnotic suggestions given covering virtually any type of situation one might encounter. The book tells how to become a professional hypnotist. It tells how to become expert at self-hypnosis all by yourself without external help. And it even contains a short dissertation going "beyond hypnosis" into the realm of psychic phenomena. There is something of value here for nearly everyone.

This book details exactly how to gain all you want to enrich your life at every level. No matter how simple or how profound your goals, this book teaches you how to realize them. The book is not magic; it is a powerful key to unlock the magic within each of us.

0-87542-300-0, 192 pgs., 5-¼ x 8, softcover $7.95

JOURNEY OF SOULS
Case Studies of Life Between Lives
by Michael Newton, Ph.D.

This remarkable book uncovers the mystery of life in the spirit world after death on earth. Dr. Michael Newton, a hypnotherapist in private practice, has developed his own hypnosis technique to reach his subjects' hidden memories of the hereafter. The narrative is woven as a progressive travel log around the accounts of 29 people who were placed in a state of superconsciousness. While in deep hypnosis, these subjects describe what has happened to them between their former reincarnations on earth. They reveal graphic details about how it feels to die, who meets us right after death, what the spirit world is really like, where we go and what we do as souls, and why we choose to come back in certain bodies.

After reading *Journey of Souls*, you will acquire a better understanding of the immortality of the human soul. Plus, you will meet day-to-day personal challenges with a greater sense of purpose as you begin to understand the reasons behind events in your own life.

1-56718-485-5, 288 pgs., 6 x 9, softcover $12.95

HOW TO UNCOVER YOUR PAST LIVES
by Ted Andrews

Knowledge of your past lives can be extremely rewarding. It can assist you in opening to new depths within your own psychological makeup. It can provide greater insight into present circumstances with loved ones, career and health. It is also a lot of fun.

Now Ted Andrews shares with you nine different techniques that you can use to access your past lives. Between techniques, Andrews discusses issues such as karma and how it is expressed in your present life; the source of past life information; soul mates and twin souls; proving past lives; the mysteries of birth and death; animals and reincarnation; abortion and pre-mature death; and the role of reincarnation in Christianity.

To explore your past lives, you need only use one or more of the techniques offered. Complete instructions are provided for a safe and easy regression. Learn to dowse to pinpoint the years and places of your lives with great accuracy, make your own self-hypnosis tape, attune to the incoming child during pregnancy, use the tarot and the cabala in past life meditations, keep a past life journal and more.

0-87542-022-2, 240 pgs., mass market, illus. $4.99

HOW TO DO AUTOMATIC WRITING
by Edain McCoy

What if someone told you the answers to nearly all of your most serious questions, deepest fears, and vexing problems could be found locked inside your own mind? And that you could tap into those resources—and all the wisdom of the ages—with little more than a pen, some paper, and a bit of practice?

The divinatory tool you can use to access this knowledge is known as automatic writing: the practice of receiving written messages channeled through your own energy and that of higher intelligence. With the help of *How to Do Automatic Writing*, in less than 60 days you can harness the powers of automatic writing to help better your life, health, finances, and spiritual endeavors.

This book offers a complete course in making automatic writing work for you. Learn who and what you can contact, how to contact them, and how to interpret the messages you receive. There is perhaps no other divination method easier to use and master than the oracle of automatic writing, and its rewards are unlimited.

1-56718-662-9, mass market, illus., 240 pp. $3.99

Prices subject to change without notice.

HOW TO MEET & WORK WITH SPIRIT GUIDES
by Ted Andrews

We often experience spirit contact in our lives but fail to recognize it for what it is. Now you can learn to access and attune to beings such as guardian angels, nature spirits and elementals, spirit totems, archangels, gods and goddesses—as well as family and friends after their physical death.

Contact with higher soul energies strengthens the will and enlightens the mind. Through a series of simple exercises, you can safely and gradually increase your awareness of spirits and your ability to identify them. You will learn to develop an intentional and directed contact with any number of spirit beings. Discover meditations to open up your subconscious. Learn which acupressure points effectively stimulate your intuitive faculties. Find out how to form a group for spirit work, use crystal balls, perform automatic writing, attune your aura for spirit contact, use sigils to contact the great archangels and much more! Read *How to Meet and Work with Spirit Guides* and take your first steps through the corridors of life beyond the physical.

0–87542–008–7, 192 pgs., mass market, illus. $4.99

HOW TO SEE AND READ THE AURA
by Ted Andrews

Everyone has an aura—the three-dimensional, shape-and-color-changing energy field that surrounds all matter. And anyone can learn to see and experience the aura more effectively. There is nothing magical about the process. It simply involves a little understanding, time, practice and perseverance.

Do some people make you feel drained? Do you find some rooms more comfortable and enjoyable to be in? Have you ever been able to sense the presence of other people before you actually heard or saw them? If so, you have experienced another person's aura. In this practical, easy-to-read manual, you receive a variety of exercises to practice alone and with partners to build your skills in aura reading and interpretation. Also, you will learn to balance your aura each day to keep it vibrant and strong so others cannot drain your vital force.

Learning to see the aura not only breaks down old barriers—it also increases sensitivity. As we develop the ability to see and feel the more subtle aspects of life, our intuition unfolds and increases, and the childlike joy and wonder of life returns.

0-87542-013-3, 160 pgs., mass market, illus. $3.95